PLATFORM PAPERS

QUARTERLY ESSAYS ON THE PERFORMING ARTS

No. 20
April 2009

CURRENCY HOUSE

PLATFORM PAPERS
Quarterly essays from Currency House Inc.
Editor: Dr John Golder, j.golder@unsw.edu.au

Currency House Inc. is a non-profit association and resource centre advocating the role of the performing arts in public life by research, debate and publication.
Postal address: PO Box 2270, Strawberry Hills, NSW 2012, Australia
Email: info@currencyhouse.org.au Tel: (02) 9319 4953
Website: www.currencyhouse.org.au Fax: (02) 9319 3649

ISBN 978-0-9805632-0-7
ISSN 1449-583X
Typeset in 10.5 Arrus BT
Printed by Griffin Digital

This edition of Platform Papers is supported by the Keir Foundation, the Greatorex Foundation, David Marr and other individual donors and advisers. To them and to all our supporters Currency House extends sincere gratitude.

Contents

AVAILABILITY *Platform Papers*, quarterly essays on the performing arts, is published every January, April, July and October and is available through bookshops or by subscription. For order form, see page 68.

LETTERS Currency House invites readers to submit letters of 400–1,000 words in response to the essays. Letters should be emailed to the Editor at info@currencyhouse.org.au or posted to Currency House at PO Box 2270, Strawberry Hills, NSW 2012, Australia. To be considered for the next issue, the letters must be received by 10 May 2009.

CURRENCY HOUSE For membership details, see our website at: www.currencyhouse.org.au

Beethoven or Britney?

The Great Divide in Music Education

ROBERT WALKER

The author

DR ROBERT WALKER has had a long career in music education. His PhD from London University was an empirical study of twentieth-century avant-garde notations and early in his career, as director of music in two selective grammar schools and an ancient cathedral school in England, he developed a curriculum which encapsulated both the western art music traditions from medieval music onwards, with the music of the twentieth-century. His students performed, studied, and composed music in these diverse styles. He has held the Chair of music education at the Universities of British Columbia and Simon Fraser in Canada before coming to the School of English, Media and Performing Arts at the University of NSW. He is the author of over a hundred research papers and eight books. He was Chief Examiner for Music and coordinator of performing arts programs for the International Baccalaureate Organisation 1987–1993, and chair of the Research Commission of the International Society for Music Education 1998–2000. He has lectured and given workshops on all continents over the last two decades and was part of an initial team to develop research in music education in South Africa among the indigenous population following the end of the apartheid era.

Author's acknowledgements

This essay draws on research which I have published, in both article and monograph form, on the background to the Western traditions in the development of classical music. I also draw on research into popular culture undertaken during my time in Canada and here in Australia. I want also to acknowledge the passionate hard work of several colleagues here in Australia who, over the years, have attempted to bring to the notice of government the 'crisis' condition of music in Australian schools. I refer particularly to Professor Gary McPherson, now of the University of Illinois, but formerly of the University of New South Wales, and the indefatigable work of Dick Letts and the Music Council of Australia.

I would also like to thank John Golder and Katharine Brisbane for their wonderful support in my attempts to make the case for school music both understandable and sensible.

1

A state of crisis

As the report of the 2005 *National Review of School Music Education* made abundantly clear,[1] music education in Australian schools is in a state of crisis, and has been for several decades.[2] Clear evidence of this fact is presented in this paper. Evidence is also presented below that not only is music an essential component of a successful education, it also has a major positive impact on performance in other subjects, especially language and mathematics, and promotes healthy attitudes to school and society at large. Research in several countries shows consistently that those who learn a musical instrument at school do better in mathematics and language than those who do not. Schools where music is important and large numbers of children participate produce better results than those with poor or no music programs. Considering the importance the Federal Government is now placing on good outcomes in school education, it is surprising that there are no signs of the Government recognizing the importance of music, and the arts generally, to the success of the overall educational enterprise in schools.

But Australia is a country which has produced some of the twentieth century's most revered composers and performers—Percy Grainger, William McKie, Barry Tuckwell, Eileen Joyce, Joan Sutherland, Richard Bonynge and Charles Mackerras, to name only a handful. These eminent musicians have all succeeded brilliantly despite the state of school music education here. Significantly, all developed their early career first through private tuition from inspiring individuals, and subsequently by going abroad to England or Europe where their talents were developed and appreciated.

Yet despite evidence of the importance of music generally for the education of all children, and such an international array of highly talented Australian musicians, school music education is described as being in dire straits, especially in the public sector and in many schools in the independent and Catholic systems which are not funded adequately for music education. Typical of the general ignorance about classical music among teenagers, for example, is the comment by a fourteen-year-old boy in a public high school in Sydney last year to one of my music education student teachers. He claimed that there was no such thing as opera in Australia: he had never heard of it. When the student teacher reminded the teenager of the Sydney Opera House, it became clear that he thought of it only as a venue for pop music and *Australian Idol*.

The main title of this essay, *Beethoven or Britney*, signifies the confusion over what should be taught in schools: classical art music of the Western traditions or popular music with which young people fill their lives outside of school. The sub-title points to an alarming disparity, described below in this essay, between a few very rich private schools that are offering a complete musical education focusing on making music—performing, composing, improvising, conducting—and the great majority of public schools which do not. Every child in these exclusive schools has the opportunity to learn about music actively, as opposed to listening passively for hours each day to the latest pop song on an iPod or the internet. The latter appears to be the main source of musical experience and default education for the vast majority of Australian children while the fortunate minority who attend schools with large and well-resourced music departments, are educated in music in the best sense of the word: learning about music as a complex expressive art form by making music themselves.

Such has been the concern of many at this state of affairs that pressure for government to do something has been building for decades. In 2004, the Music Council of Australia, the Australian Society for Music Education, and many other groups and individuals including Chris Pearce, Member for Knox, Victoria, and a former musician, finally persuaded the Federal Government to conduct an enquiry into the state of music education in Australian schools. In March 2004, Dr Brendan Nelson, then Minister for Education, and Rodney Kemp, Minister for the Arts, jointly announced a national review of school music education. The final report was delivered to Minister Nelson in November 2005.

In her letter to the Minister presenting the *Review* findings, Professor Margaret Seares, Chair of the Steering Committee, made it very clear that there were serious issues to be addressed, and that music education was essential to all young Australians:

> This Review has made the case for the importance of music in Australian schools. It has shown the importance and significance of music in the education of all young Australians and therefore asserts its inalienable place in all Australian schools.
>
> [...W]hile [...] submissions [...] revealed some fine examples of school music programmes, they also reveal cycles of neglect and inequity which impacts [*sic*] to the detriment of too many young Australians [...] The research has revealed [...] significant variability in the quality of teaching [and] detrimental impacts arising from changes in the place of music within the overall curriculum. Overall, the quality of music in schools is patchy at best and reform is demonstrably needed, with strong support from your Government.
>
> Raising the quality and status of music education will have a positive impact on the breadth and depth of aesthetic, cognitive, social and experiential learning for all Australian students and ultimately for our society at large. (Foreword, p. iii)

On its opening pages the *Review* lists some startlingly critical findings:

- Many Australian students miss out on effective music education because of lack of equity of access, lack of quality provision; and the poor status of music in many schools.

- Music education in Australian schools is at a critical point where prompt action is needed to right the inequalities in school music.
- Music-specific professional development is urgently required for generalist classroom [primary] teachers currently in schools.
- Hours for pre-service teacher education for music have contracted radically in the last ten years and do not adequately prepare generalist primary teachers for teaching music in schools. Urgent action is needed to address this problem. (pp. v-vi)

The report contains many such statements, all pointing to what the *Review* identifies as a crisis. But when asked by the *Australian* newspaper in December 2005 about the role of popular music in education, Professor Seares replied succinctly: she could see no reason why children should not learn about Britney Spears as well as Beethoven.

This was not a constructive comment, since the *Review* had pointed so tellingly to the inadequate training of teachers in music, especially at primary school level. In her letter to the Minister, Professor Seares asserted the importance of the aesthetic and cognitive value of music to young Australians. The implication of this remark, however, seems to be that she finds little difference, in terms of aesthetic and cognitive value, between Beethoven's and Britney Spears' music. It is puzzling, to say the least. But this issue of what music should be taught, and why, is central to the curriculum; it demands a clear distinction be made between entertainment and education.

This distinction is dangerously blurred. The research referred to above, and described in more detail below, is clear: putting hard discipline into learning to play a musical instrument and singing has clear benefits for schoolwork generally. Music for fun or entertainment does not.

The recommendations listed in the *Review* were quite specific and cover many important aspects, which require a broader platform than this one. I want to focus on three of the most pressing problems defined by the *Review*, and which have been well known for some time—*lack of resources and equipment; lack of musical knowledge and pedagogical expertise among generalist primary school teachers; and lack of clarity with regard to music curriculum content*. Each of these is embedded in complex issues which emanate from outside the discipline of music, but which hold sway over those who have responsibility for the organisation, management and maintenance of school music in all its aspects. Presently, I shall turn to each of these and consider the impact generally on educational thinking, policy and implementation by the rise of sociologically-based theory and practice in education. But first let us look at some examples from across the world about the beneficial effects of good quality music education on children's learning and development.

The beneficial effects of music

In 1999 a longitudinal study of over 25,000 high-school students led by American education researcher James Catterall of the University of California, found that students who played musical instruments from an early age had significantly higher mathematics test scores in their final year of high school than those who did not.[3] Interestingly, the effect was more noticeable in students from lower, rather than higher, senior secondary education backgrounds. The study also found benefits for reading and more positive attitudes towards social inclusivity from participation in any arts program.

The Arts Education Partnership (AEP) of Washington D.C. also provides some compelling evidence demonstrating beneficial effects on school achievement of all the arts, but especially music. The AEP produced a Compendium of scientific studies reporting these effects. Three main themes are listed indicating important findings:

1. Meta-analysis studies based in large bodies of research over the last few decades reveal consistently strong, positive relationships between music and learning in other subjects.
2. Generative neurological and cognitive frameworks for learning transfer have emerged from research on music and learning.
3. There is an underlying tension between the 'one-way cause and effect' and the 'two-way interaction' models of research on music and learning.[4]

Research papers reviewed in this Compendium support a more interactive model of learning in and through music. Meta-analysis indicates that there is a strong and reliable association between study of music and performance on standardised reading and verbal tests. The 'two-way interactionist' position is that improvement in learning in either of two disciplines—taught separately or together—suggests that one discipline catalyzes, reinforces, and deepens learning in the other. Thus research now offers a theoretical basis for, and growing evidence of, the significant effects of learning shared between music and other measures of academic achievement.[5]

Takako Fujioka, of the Baycrest Rotman Research Institute in Toronto, studied several thousand children and the effects of playing music instruments on their general learning and development. He comments:

> Our work explores how musical training affects the way in which the brain develops. It is clear that music is good for children's cognitive development and that music should be part of the school curriculum, especially at pre-school and primary levels.[6]

Laurel Trainor, professor of psychology, neuroscience and behaviour at McMaster University, and Director of the McMaster Institute for Music and the Mind, is conducting another study on the effects of music on development. She comments:

> It is very interesting that the children taking music lessons improved more over the year on general memory skills that are correlated with non-musical abilities such as literacy, verbal memory, visio-spatial processing, mathematics and IQ than did children not taking lessons. It suggests that musical training is having an effect on how the brain gets wired for general cognitive functioning related to memory and attention.[7]

The Music Council of Australia website lists a number of similar studies being carried out world-wide, all of which point to the same conclusion: that serious music-learning affects general cognitive functioning, which in turn has a beneficial effect on learning language and mathematics, and studies in general.[8]

A recent study by Northwestern University researchers, to be published in the April 2009 issue of *Nature Neuroscience*, suggests that Mom was right when she insisted that we continue with our music lessons—even after it became clear that they were not going to lead to a professional career.[9] The study is the first to provide concrete evidence that playing a musical instrument significantly enhances the brainstem's sensitivity to speech sounds, a finding which has broad implications, because it applies to sound-encoding skills involved not only in music, but also in language. The findings indicate that experience with music at a young age can, in effect, 'fine-tune' the brain's auditory system: 'Increasing music experience appears to benefit all children—whether musically exceptional or not—in a wide range of learning activities,' says Nina Kraus, director of Northwestern's Auditory Neuroscience Laboratory and senior author of the study.

Professor Kraus states that 'there is concrete evidence that playing music can significantly enhance the brain and sharpen hearing for all kinds of sounds, including speech. [...] Experience with music appears to help with many other things in life, potentially transferring to activities like reading, picking up tones of voices or hearing sounds in a noisy classroom—all important for learning languages.'

> We've found that by playing music—an action thought of as a function of the neocortex—a person

> may actually be tuning the brainstem. This suggests that the relationship between the brainstem and neocortex is a dynamic and reciprocal one and tells us that our basic sensory circuitry is more malleable than we previously thought.

A study undertaken last year in Switzerland by Olive Wetter and colleagues of the University of Zurich compared 53 children who practised music with 67 children who did not.[10] Overall average marks as well as average marks of all school subjects except sports were significantly higher in the group performing music than the group which was not.

The British government has recently begun to take notice of this overwhelming evidence of the importance of playing music to child development and school success. In 2005, the Qualifications and Curriculum Authority (QCA) curriculum on-line[11] justified the arts in education by the following:

> Investing in the arts can transform schools. The arts can raise standards, change attitudes, improve behaviour and increase the quality of teaching and learning[12]

In January 2007 Education Secretary Alan Johnson announced a £10m package of measures to boost music education, with an emphasis on singing. Composer Howard Goodall, named Singing Ambassador, will lead the Government's national singing campaign in primary schools. Arrangements will be made for choir schools attached to cathedral and collegiate choirs to work with children in their area. 'As well as being a worthwhile activity for its own sake,' said Minister

Johnson, 'music is a powerful learning tool which can build children's confidence, teamwork, and language skills.'[13]

In January, 2009, David Miliband, Schools Standards Minister, echoed Johnson's words. 'Music teaching is central to improving educational achievement,' he said,[14] while announcing a £1.5m funding increase for music services in England. Music, he added 'helped self-confidence and motivation among pupils'. Thirteen local education authorities in England had so far participated in pilot schemes which involved professional musicians giving lessons to children aged up to 11, he said. Another scheme for promoting music in schools was announced by the Music Manifesto group, involving three government departments in the UK, including the Department for Children, Schools and Families. Up to £10m is to be made available over the period 2009–11 to fund projects which develop or extend music activity for young people delivered through partnerships which should include at least one local authority.[15]

This overwhelming evidence is in the public domain and readily available to our Australian decision-makers. Meanwhile, we struggle with the present lamentable state of music in the nation's schools. What follows is discussion of some of the commentary and public debate aroused by the *National Review of School Music Education*.

2

Review finding 1: Inadequate resources

Lack of equipment and facilities is easily one of the most pressing problems, in respect of which the *Review* makes the following recommendations for the three levels of government:

1. The Australian Government should provide one-off grants to schools for music facilities and equipment, including instruments.
2. State/Territory school systems and sectors should ensure that schools have up-to-date and well-maintained facilities and equipment to support contemporary music programs.
3. Communities and parents should support music in schools through fundraising and advocating for funds, facilities and equipment. (p. 130)

Importantly, a close look at the *Review*'s findings reveals a serious disparity of provision between public schools in general and a small number of well-endowed private schools rich in resources and equipment. The *Review* offers ample evidence of this, particularly in what it called the 'Armidale cluster'.

The *Review* panel decided, sensibly, to select a few areas and to focus on just twenty locations which could be considered typical of the way in which school music is provided across the country. Armidale, in northern New South Wales, was one of the chosen towns. This university town, with a population of around 20,000, is unique in that it has a long tradition of highly successful youth orchestras, choirs, music festivals, competitions and concerts. Together with three major private schools, New England Girls School (NEGS), Presbyterian Ladies College (PLC), and The Armidale School (TAS), it has two publicly-funded high schools, Armidale High School and Duval High School. For some reason, the *Review* made no reference to NEGS, which is surprising considering the school's strong music component. All these schools are proud of the music programs they offer and of the high musical standards achieved in their student performances. There can be no doubt that the schools, both pupils and staff, individually and collaboratively, make an enormous contribution to the success of Armidale's musical enterprise as a whole. As the *Review* makes clear, Armidale is a unique centre for youth music-making—and this is in large measure due to the musical activities of its schools.

However, despite this high commendation, comments on music resources and facilities in the four schools to which the *Review* did refer reveal alarming differences. Teachers at Armidale High stated that 'lack of resources (rooms, equipment and performance venues) [...] creates difficulties'. Duval students are obliged to share facilities with PLC, where the music staff 'willingly share their specialist music facilities'. And talented Duval students share in the Sydney Conservatorium of Music Outreach Programs, which are run by PLC. The resources at Armidale High are described as 'relatively limited, with two music classrooms, a small amount of music technology equipment, and a single storeroom [...] with no window, used as a practice room'. Armidale High students also share PLC and TAS facilities and activities such as the Sydney Conservatorium Outreach Programs (p. 172).

By contrast, the *Review* describes PLC as 'well-resourced, with two large specialist music rooms (including a grand piano and many other instruments), practice rooms and a music technology lab'. Music has the largest budget of all in the school, and performance programs start in the infants' sector of the school, to include orchestra, string orchestra, wind bands, jazz groups, and many other ensembles. Choir is compulsory for all students and the *Review* lists several specialist choirs (p. 172). Resources at TAS are described as 'a purpose-specific music wing with two large classrooms, practice rooms, a large ensemble room, and a well-equipped music technology lab' (p. 173).

According to one Duval High School student, 'It's really the wealthier people who have more options [...] and it is only people who can have private music lessons outside of school that do music' (p. 172). And a student at Armidale High stated that 'you have got to have a bit of each [. . .], private music lessons then the school thing and large community groups, to get a full range of experiences' (p. 171).

No such comments came from students at the two private schools: private music lessons are supplied by the school as part of the fee structure paid by parents. Clearly, a major reason for the success of the Armidale cluster is due to the resources and support systems for music invested by the private schools and the way these are shared with the two public schools. The teachers in all the Armidale schools receive high praise for their expertise, enthusiasm and dedication. However, without appropriate facilities and resources, these assets are not enough; it is hard to avoid the conclusion that as far as music resources are concerned in Armidale the public sector is being generously subsidised by the private sector.

The *Review* panel was impressed by these co-operative arrangements, which they also found to be in place in Melbourne. They suggest that 'the site visits, notably the Armidale cluster and [Melbourne's] Xavier College [...] showed the value of collaboration between schools as a further way of developing effective music programs. This is a trend to be encouraged.' (*Review*, p. 130) The proposition that richly-resourced private schools share their resources with local publicly-funded schools is an interesting one, but hardly a long-term solution. It represents an abrogation of government responsibility to the public sector.

The *Review*'s account of resources in two public high schools as compared with two private schools exemplifies a nation-wide situation. In Armidale we have one of our most musical communities, yet resources in the public schools are still described as inadequate compared to those in the private schools. If this is the situation in Armidale, what chance is there for adequate public-school resources in less supportive communities? None of the other nineteen locations and schools examined by the *Review* offer better grounds for optimism.

These figures provide conclusive evidence that there exists in Australian schools a form of musical apartheid, where a small number of rich and well-supported private schools are comparatively lavishly resourced compared to the overwhelming majority in the public sector. This is contributing to a growing trend towards the private sector by parents seeking quality for their children. Directors of music in those Sydney private schools with large and highly active music departments freely admit that the desire for a strong music program is one reason why parents choose their school. Many teachers have read the research reports about the beneficial effects on mathematics and language development of learning to play and instrument, and they see in their results how essential music is to a good education.

The growth in the number of students entering the private sector became particularly evident between 2000 and 2007. According to the website of the Independent Schools Council of Australia (ISCA), in 2000 students in non-government schools across Australia accounted for 30.8% (or 999,138 individuals) of the total student population.[16] By 2007, however, that percentage had grown to 33.6 (1,148,146 individuals), compared with 66.4 (2,268,377) in the public sector. In 2007, for example, 34.8% of South Australia's students attended private schools. The figure in Victoria was 35.7, in NSW 33.5, and in the ACT over 40%. However, as I have insisted, not all private schools can boast the kind of music resources of TAS and PLC—but some can, and they attract parents accordingly.

The ISCA website shows that only 17% of secondary students in the private sector currently go to independent schools and only a small fraction of this number are lucky enough to go to schools with excellent music programs and facilities. A further 22% of secondary students go to Catholic schools, many of which are not well resourced for music.

No precise figures are available for the number of musically well-endowed private secondary schools across the country. However, bearing in mind the Armidale model of public and private schools supporting each other's music programs, some exemplary extrapolations might be made from data concerning Sydney schools. In total, there are 200 publicly-funded secondary schools in the metropolitan area compared with around 170 independent high schools of varying types, including some combined schools.[17] Of the latter I can identify around 30 schools with first-class facilities, resources and equipment. Some are extremely lavish, with multiple music classrooms, large concert halls with a full-size concert grand piano and numerous practice rooms. Several have a school chapel with a large concert pipe organ, and one has an opera hall.[18] Most have several orchestras, beginning with infant instrumentalists', and award-winning choirs, many instrumental groups, including pop and rock music, wind bands, jazz orchestras, and concert bands. All have large numbers of music teachers on staff, both full-time and part-time. Several employ full-time composers on term contracts to work with the children.

Ignoring the one publicly-funded special music high school attached to the Sydney Conservatorium, there are very few—if any—state high schools that are able to compete with such resources. However ready and willing governors, staff and parents might be to do so, it beggars belief that these 30 or so schools in the independent sector might be able to provide adequate support for 200 public schools, by sharing their resources and equipment. Moreover, the idea of this kind of collaboration sends a mixed message to government from the *Review*, which simultaneously castigates government for its neglect of music resources and equipment in its publicly funded schools and at the same time suggests that public schools should make use of the facilities available in the private sector!

To date there has been no response from the Federal Government concerning the grossly inadequate state of music resources. Music has not so far been included in the national curriculum at present under construction. Let us hope that some of the $14.7 billion for school buildings in the Federal Government's recession-busting $42 billion stimulus package, will go to music-making utilities.

3

Review finding 2: Poor primary teaching

The next major problem is the lack of musical training in generalist primary-school teachers. This leads to poor primary teaching, and a knock-on effect in secondary schools: most children enter secondary school at Grade 7 with little or no musical knowledge or understanding, with the result that for many there are few alternatives to pop music.

Of the several factors that contribute to the lack of competence in music education among primary teachers, the most urgent is the need to address the drastic reduction in music and music pedagogy programs in university pre-service degrees for generalist primary school teachers. Anxious for decision-makers to hear this 'key message', the *Review* called for 'urgent action' to be taken in order 'to address this problem' (p. vi).

Except for Queensland, no state or territory acknowledges, or employs, primary school teachers as specialists: all are generalists expected to teach the whole spectrum of subjects to K–6 students. This is a long-standing issue, and the *Review* acknowledges the fact, citing published research on the topic from as far back as the 1960s. And it recommends that all states follow Queensland's example and allow specialist music teachers to be designated as such in their qualifications and employed as such (*Review*, pp. xii & xvi).

The Dawkins reforms of the late 1980s implemented the same changes to teacher-training in Australia as had occurred during the 1960s in Canada and the 1970s in the UK. In Australia, Colleges of Advanced Education (CAE), originally established primarily for the training of teachers, ceased to exist—and all teacher-training was transferred to the university sector. Many professional staff of the CAE found their new life difficult: they did not fit into the university thinking or milieu. They found that they were expected now to base their work on theory and research—whereas previously they had been expert by virtue of experience and practice. While to those who administered and ran the system, this may have appeared to be a move in the right direction, it destroyed the wealth of practical experience built up in the colleges. But most radically, it compelled practitioners to become theorists, which ultimately proved detrimental to the educational enterprise. Professional practice became essentially theory-based rather than experience-based. For music teaching this was disastrous, as the 2003 Stevens Report pointed out. Stevens discovered that 'pre-service teachers [in the new university setting], many possessing very limited musical experience or background, received on average only 23 hours of music in their entire teacher-education program' (cited in *Review*, p. 15). Intending teachers need experience with live children making music in school settings rather than theories about child-learning or music pedagogy.

The *Review* goes on to cite an unpublished 2005 survey by the Australian Association for Research in Music Education, entitled 'Music in Primary Teacher Education', which reported similar findings regarding 30 Australian university teacher-education degree programs (*Review*, p. 15). Rachel Hocking provides clearer data in a more recent survey of 30 university pre-service primary teacher education programs.[19] The percentages of time in pre-service primary degrees devoted to music in these universities reported by Hocking are frankly alarming. They range from 0.0% in the Australian Catholic University to 4.6% at Monash University. Eight universities devote less than 1%, another nine devote between 1% and 2%, three devote between 2% and 3.1%, while only Tasmania and Monash show above 4%. All the universities surveyed (except the Australian Catholic University) have mandatory arts programs, in which dance, drama, music and visual arts are taught as a single subject. Course-work time for 'the arts as a whole' ranges between 2% and 6% over the complete degree. Tasmania (12.5%) and Western Sydney (16.6%) are the only universities showing above 10% devoted to 'the arts'.

With such minimal training these teachers are expected to be able to teach music, drama, dance, and visual arts to children from Kindergarten to Grade 6, as well as all the other subjects—maths, English, science, etc. Each of these arts subjects is an independent type of expression with little in common either in historical or contemporary practice. Each requires different sense perceptions in developing understanding and mastery. And each is different in the mental and physical skill required to be active in them. Moreover, to achieve even a minimal level of skill many hours of devoted practice are required. It would be better if these universities focused on just one or two subjects, in a program that could do justice to the discipline, rather than attempt the impossible with such inadequate contact hours. But this is part of a much larger debate, that of curriculum and the rise of sociological theories influencing teacher education, which I address in some detail below.

Triumph of theory over practice

Having worked as a teacher-educator of both primary and secondary teachers throughout my career in universities in England, Canada and Australia, I can confidently assert that the problem with primary pre-service training is common to all three countries. They all rely on the same sources of theory, scholarship, and research. The idea of merging visual art, music, drama, and dance into one subject—the arts—emerged during the 1970s and spread across the English-speaking world. It is not found in either Continental European countries, or in Asia.

Educational theorists were the driving force, and they saw things only through the lens of sociology. The motivation was often altruistic in the sense that the desire was to remove elitism from the provision of and attitude to the arts, and to produce a more democratic and caring society. In effect, instead of offering the highest level of educational experience and opportunity to all students, irrespective of their social or ethnic background, the result was to reduce content and pedagogy to the lowest common denominator. As combined arts programs in universities proliferated, sociological issues grew in influence over the traditions of the single art form. A huge divide appeared between what the universities were teaching and what many state and territory curriculum documents claimed to teach.

For example, university pre-service music programs for primary teachers, as reported by Rachel Hocking, are all designated as 'arts' or 'creative arts' (plural). However, most state curricula specify individual subjects, such as music, visual arts, drama, and dance. Many, but not all, state and territory curriculum documents for Kindergarten to Grade 6 also describe the arts subjects and the expected outcomes individually. However, universities which offer pre-service training to primary school teachers do not, it seems, teach the arts as separate subjects. There is, therefore, a serious disjunction between what universities are producing in their pre-service primary-teacher programs and what most individual state and territories are advocating in their curriculum documents. The New South Wales Creative Arts Curriculum K–6 document, for instance, lists each subject separately, as it does the outcomes for each subject.[20] Yet the *Review* clearly documents the mixed approach in universities to arts teaching for pre-service primary schools citing both the Stevens Report and the unpublished 2005 survey mentioned above. This creates confusion in the system.

All thirty universities cited in the Hocking study list compulsory combined or integrated 'Arts' components in their primary education degrees. In all of them music is a small component: for example, one-seventh of the combined arts program at Flinders, one-fifth at Central Queensland, Curtin, Charles Darwin, a quarter at Deakin, Wollongong, and Southern Cross. By contrast, most state curricula set out individual outcomes and indicators for each single subject. Nowhere in the New South Wales Curriculum documents (Creative Arts K–6 Syllabus[21]) is there any reference to multiple arts teaching. The outcomes and indicators, as well as general content overviews, all list each subject independently and separately. The same is true in Victoria and Queensland. In Western Australia the arts subjects appear heavily linked throughout the K–12 program.[22] There is little indicating progression of skills and cognitive understanding, and page 73 of the WA Curriculum Framework explains that 'assessment should not discriminate and should be sensitive to differences such as gender, ethnicity, language, race and socio-economic circumstances'.[23] In effect there does not appear to be any objective assessment throughout the whole program which has legitimacy beyond the boundaries of WA. But perhaps the most significant aspect of all the music curriculum documents lies in their use of concepts, processes and strategies rather than required musical texts.

The NSW curriculum documents in music dealing with K–10 (Creative Arts K–6 Syllabus, and Music Mandatory and Elective Courses for Years 7–10, published by the NSW Board of Studies) are couched throughout in concepts and strategies. There is not one piece of music listed which all students need to study. This lack of prescribed texts means that some children can be brought up entirely on Western art music, others on the Beatles, or on any music the teacher feels inclined to teach. This is no framework for education, rather a recipe for encouraging personal bias and group allegiances. The Western Australian curriculum is equally vague in its musical content, allowing any music at the teacher's discretion to be taught throughout. Nowhere is there any specific piece or genre of music named as having significance of any kind.

The Queensland curriculum documents, on the other hand, are quite explicit on the context of learning, the educative processes, and the elements of music to be covered.[24] These are based on the UK model of listening and analyzing repertoire, composing and performing. Assessment is rigorous and clearly explained. In the senior grades, while no specific compositions are listed, those students specialising in music with the intention of going on to tertiary level, have prescribed content under the sub-heading 'structure'. 'Cantata, song cycles, sonata, symphony, suite, and concerto' are listed. This is the nearest we get to a specific genre of music—i.e., Western classical art music. Similar prescriptions can be found in the Grades 11 and 12 curriculum documents in NSW. The Victorian and South Australian curriculum documents are similar with a focus on elements, concepts, structures, and perceptual processes, but no specific compositions.

As the *Review* implies, there is little uniformity across the country in terms of curriculum content, except for the common usage of generic sonic elements such as sound concepts, structures, rhythm, melody, timbre, and uses of music in various social contexts. All offer a pathway at Grade 12 for those wishing to go on to study music at university, but NSW has an additional pathway for those who just want to study music, any music, but do not wish to go on to tertiary level.

All curriculum documents are heavily infected with sociological goals, especially involving music in daily life, music within cultural contexts without being specific, and music which has cultural significance, again without definition. But there is little in any of the documentation to explain what this might mean in terms of the musical elements used, or the socio-cultural context within which the music is performed, or what connections might exist between musical elements and cultural context, or certainly what it might mean in classroom practice. There is a void between the over-arching aims of the music curriculum concerning developing cultural awareness, and the specific musical elements and concepts (such as pitch, rhythm, etc.) which make up the nitty-gritty of what teachers are supposed to teach. A Scottish or Irish folk song, for example, is not studied in its historical context linking the melody or rhythm to Scottish or Irish lifestyles. Instead, the melody is regarded as a phenomenon illustrating pitch use, and so on with rhythm.

Without doubt, the idea of music in its cultural context is a crucial part of a music education since it has great significance for both understanding and performance of the work. But these documents offer little evidence that anything substantial occurs within this aspect of musical study. I shall turn later to a consideration of what cultural context means, and argue why it is important for all children, everywhere—but especially here in Australia—to learn about it. First, however, I want to show how the impact of sociological thinking on education has made it difficult, if not impossible, to mount an argument based on musical thinking.

4

Review finding 3: Detrimental curriculum changes

During the 1970s educational theory and practice took an important new direction as new sociological perspectives began to be applied to education. The epistemological focus in curriculum changed from that of the discipline of music to the sociological issue of how people used such music in their daily lives.[25] Suddenly, it was not music, *per se*, that mattered, but what people did with it. Music became a different subject, and all music was accorded equal value. What mattered was how, why, and in what circumstances people heard or listened to musical sounds, be they Mozart, Led Zeppelin, Inuit throat music, African drumming, Indonesian gamelan music or the Beatles. The notion of music as an art disappeared in the face of music as a commodity. This created a dilemma for music education and for the notion of an education generally: what was there to teach about music?

Several sources of sociological theory had an impact on educational thinking. Two of these were of particular importance—Pierre Bourdieu, in France, who argued that schools as currently structured were agents for perpetuating class divisions,[26] and the Birmingham Group of cultural theorists in the UK, who argued for popular culture to be recognized by society in general and by education in particular.[27] Others, such as Brazilian philosopher and educationist Paulo Freire, argued for education to be made available, not simply to a privileged few, but to all the oppressed peoples of the world.[28] Knowledge itself was seen as linked to class and status, and so had to be modified to permit access by society's dispossessed and marginalised. These ideas spread rapidly: the plight of the poor and lower classes in Western countries became for many a *cause célèbre*; and current educational structures and knowledge were regarded as instruments of oppression.

In one sense these aims were laudable: they were intended to empower those whom the rigid social and political structures of Western society had rendered marginal. The idea that schools could also be agents for change was refreshing and new. One problem, however, lay in the fact that the type of change for which schools were supposed to be agents was never defined. Nor, apart from getting rid of schools altogether, or replacing formal schooling with home-schooling, how we might achieve these socio-political goals.[29] Nevertheless, by the 1980s this movement had gained immense leverage in government and among policy-makers.

I recall my time as a high-school teacher in the UK during the late 1960s and 1970s, when the British government abolished the 11-plus selection examination, and with it selective teaching.[30] I was teaching in an élite selective high school and was in favour of this change, being genuinely concerned for the 75% of children who were then condemned by the examination to attend non-selective schools which were notoriously under-staffed and under-resourced. I felt that this dramatic organisational change might improve the educational experience for all children. However, this idea quickly lost its attraction.

First, and foremost, the notion that the academic staff transferred from the selective high schools would, as the government intimated, raise the academic and educational standards of the new comprehensive schools, quickly dissipated. The reason was partly that the government did not immediately abolish all selective high schools, leaving quite a few who fought and eventually won their battle to retain their status. This meant that many highly-educated academic staff could remain in such schools. But, at the same time, the government increased the number of universities in the UK, thus providing many jobs out of the school sector for well-qualified staff from the soon-to-be-defunct selective high schools.

The latter was the route I took out of school teaching during this turbulent period. Experience in applying for posts in the new comprehensive schools made me quickly realize that many of these newly-formed high schools would in fact become repositories of mediocrity, partly because of a lack of resources, but mainly because of the new ideas emerging from sociology and cultural theory.[31] Many in these new comprehensive schools regarded the traditional disciplines as helping to maintain the socio-economic *status quo* in all its unfairness and inequality: if society was to be rendered more equal and inclusive, knowledge itself would have to be changed. They saw the abolition of the 11-plus examination as a clarion call for social change through education.

While I was all in favour of raising standards of equality and inclusiveness, the idea that for socio-political reasons epistemology itself needed radically re-designing seemed to me absurd. And I think it can be fairly said that today, despite all the attempts since the 1970s to use schools as agents of change through new structures of learning, virtually no social or economic progress of the oppressed has been effected anywhere through this modus operandi. North American Aboriginals and African-Americans, like their Australian counterparts, have gained nothing, and neither have poorer classes in deprived homes across the nation: illiteracy and poor school achievement, leading to unemployment, crime and drugs have not disappeared. It was doomed from the start and so it has proved to be. The successful schemes are those that educate children in the mainstream skills and knowledge of society.[32]

Multi-literacies

It was from these sociological beginnings that more sophisticated attempts to radically alter education in schools have emerged during the 1990s and into the first years of the twenty-first century. In this country, these became known, first, under the banner of such inclusive terminology as 'multi-literacies'. The Australian development began in earnest with a seminal paper published in the *Harvard Educational Review* by several Australians, rising academics who are now deans or heads of education faculties in several of our universities.[33] Its title, significantly, was 'A pedagogy of multi-literacies: designing social futures'. The political intent implied by the subtitle signified the tone of the paper. And the authors quickly began to influence teacher education and state curriculum documents in the directions suggested. This movement then developed into what became known as 'critical literacy' affecting predominantly the teaching of language and other humanities subjects.[34] In the past decade the Australian Research Council has funded many research projects involving universities and schools implementing these ideas in the classroom and curriculum documents.[35]

The motivations were similar to those of the 1960s and 1970s: to bring in people from the margins and to enable them to take their proper place in society.

This time, however, it was more clearly aimed at the whole population of children. Unfortunately, these more recent moves, like their predecessors, failed. They failed because of the weakness of the case they argued. Bringing in people from the margins so that they can fully engage in society is, one hopes, a basic aim of a civilized society. But changing the *epistemological* basis of mainstream knowledge —i.e., to dumb down to a level which is thought to be of benefit to those marginalized—is not the way to do it. Inclusion, incorporation, and full involvement in mainstream society are the only means by which every citizen will be enabled to achieve his or her true potential through education. But this requires heavy investment and political commitment from government, from business and from society at large. Prime Minister Rudd and Education Minister Julia Guillard have placed great emphasis on the fundamental value of education in their public promises of an 'education revolution' since election in 2007; but apart from an undertaking to distribute computers to every schoolchild, so far there has been no sign of this occurring.

If such movements have generally failed to make direct impact on music education, it is because, unlike language, music is not denotative. One cannot easily assign political motivations to musical melody, rhythm or harmony in the way one can to words in language. Nonetheless, the same sociologically- and politically-based criticism of musical epistemology occurred through the valorization of popular culture and its music as a proper focus in music education. Popular music, its sources among the uneducated and oppressed, was seen as an educational panacea, because it eradicated the alienation supposedly caused by Western art music, the music, traditionally, of privilege and authority. This theme was taken up by a number of music educators across Australia from the late 1980s onwards. Their success is evident in the licence many state music curriculum documents give teachers to compile their own syllabus.

However, sociological arguments for inclusion or exclusion do not in themselves constitute sufficient justification for application to a subject like music. Claims that popular music is accessible to all, and ubiquitous in everyday life, might have sociological validity, but not necessarily educational or musical validity. The latter requires more rigorous justification. Knowledge cannot easily be used as a sociological tool, as many have mistakenly thought. The laws of physics are universal: they do not change according to the user. This applies to all forms of knowledge, but there are important differences between logical and empirical forms of knowledge in the sciences and mathematics, and the expressive forms invented by human societies. In the case of the former, tests for verification ensure objectivity. With the latter it is to long-standing cultural traditions that we turn. Music is one form of expression which has validity only within the context of a cultural tradition. The global entertainment media, however intrusive and powerful, do not constitute a cultural tradition.

The power of culture, including the traditions, beliefs, behaviour, loyalties, and ways of thinking into which one is born, penetrate very deeply into our psyche. They can never really be eradicated or replaced by popular entertainment.[36] Despite this, the new forces for change in school curricula considered that they had found strong support in the music of the entertainment world. It was the music of the people, and—most important of all from the point of view of education—it was the music that captured young people for many hours each and every day. Thus, adolescence and popular culture were incorporated into the case being argued and the music of popular culture became a major component.

But there is an even stronger case for including Western art music in everyone's education. First and foremost, while I am far from suggesting that it cannot be entertaining, education is not entertainment. Education is concerned with developing knowledge and expertise through a process which demands hard work, dedicated practice and commitment to master skills and develop understanding. This is no less true of music than of any other art form. We have already noted the extensive evidence of physical and psychological benefits that derive from a child's music education. But it is equally important that the child's music education program be challenging.

5

The central importance of Western art music

It is therefore not just any music learning that enhances general school achievement. Research has shown that learning to play Western classical music on an instrument, or to sing it with appropriate training, has a significant effect on language and mathematics learning, and on general school functioning. The reason lies in the structure of most Western classical music: the system of harmony, melody, and musical form, such as sonatas, fugues, etc., developed over hundreds of years. Additionally, there are some very important expressive attributes of Western art music which address some basic questions of the human predicament, and exemplify cultural ways of thinking in the West. But one of the most important aspects of this music is the high level of technical skill required to perform it and to understand it. In so many ways our state and territories curriculum documents sidestep acknowledgement of this hard work and dedication. The *National Review of School Music Education* does not even mention the importance of focused practice to achievement. The implication is that music, any music, is good for students. This is not supported by the enormous amount of research on the effects of music education on school achievement: only focused practice has such beneficial effects. Just playing around with pop music, for example, is of no discernible benefit to general school performance.

In Australia one would not find such an attitude in sport. The Australian Institute of Sport in Canberra proudly describes its athletes as élite and requires nothing less than total commitment to the acquisition of a solid and superior technique. Music is no different. However, even in the world of pop music technical ability is essential. The *Australian Idol* competition results demonstrate that those who have been professionally taught to perform, often starting with Western art music, have the best chance of success.[37]

Western art music is not, as some might maintain, a matter of musical truth or superiority over other types of music, but rather a means of gaining understanding of how humans in Western society have, over two millennia, come to interpret their place in the scheme of things. All thinking is to some extent cultural, whatever the cultural context, and developing understanding of the traditions of Western art music is closely linked to developing understanding of Western culture. There are ethical, moral, and complex psychological lessons to be learned from this music. In other words, Western music contains the essence of Western cultural thinking about life, love, war, politics, and above all what it means to be human. How it does this is what education should be about. And I imply here education for *all* children. Indeed, many countries now subscribe to this view and include Western classical music in their curricula.

The evidence from Asia, for example, is that in Korea, Japan, China, Taiwan, and Singapore, Western art music is a major part of the education of all children, together with the music of their own culture. Specific pieces of Western art music are listed in curriculum books used in schools in these countries, and children are expected to know and learn about these pieces as they progress through school.[38] One illustration of how effective this is can be seen in the popularity of the Korean pop group Shinhua, who sell more recordings in Asia than any Western pop group. One of their most popular songs in 2004 was 'Twinkling of Paradise'. Its theme was taken from Tchaikowsky's ballet *Swan Lake*, the *Entr'acte*, already familiar to most of these young people from school; and in concerts all over Asia the audience joined in the singing. In China it is estimated that over ten million Chinese children are learning the piano by performing the Western repertoire.

One reason why Western art music is so popular in Asia—consider how many of the world's famous classical musicians now are Asian—is that it is so challenging, so profound and so rewarding to try and master in performance. This was the message brought by Sheila Melvin and Jingdong Cai from China.[39] Many Chinese preferred Western classical music to Chinese traditional opera for these reasons. And witness the amazing results on the world of Western classical music of the graduates of the Beijing Conservatorium of Music.

Even more startling is the Venezuelan Youth Orchestra scheme. *El Sistema*, as the program is popularly called, is currently celebrating over 30 years of making classical musicians out of half-a-million young Venezuelans. It has transformed the lives of many underprivileged and at-risk youths in the process. Such renowned musicians as the Berlin Philharmonic conductors Sir Simon Rattle and Claudio Abbado, and the great operatic tenor Placido Domingo, have wept at the beauty of the playing of these young orchestras from Venezuela. *El Sistema* has brought the sounds of Beethoven to the masses by giving children instruments, scholarships, and free transportation for the lowest economic classes in the country. 'In Venezuela, we broke the myth that you have to be from the upper class to play the violin,' says Carlos Sedan, director of the school in Sarria, a destitute and violent area of Caracas.[40] And very recently, a very young conductor from the Venezuela Youth Orchestral traditions was appointed conductor of the Los Angeles Philharmonic Orchestra. Today Venezuala boasts 200 youth orchestras, the product of *El Sistema*.

Another inspiring example is that of the West-Eastern Divan Orchestra, a youth orchestra which was the inspiration of the Israeli pianist and conductor Daniel Barenboim and the Palestinian writer, the late Edward Said. Their mission was to break down the barriers between Israel and Palestine and they first gathered in Weimar 1999. Today they continue to risk the hazards of playing in Ramallah and other Palestinian territories. Here is a quotation from a young Israeli:

> Noa, now 23, had six days notice for her audition for the Divan in 2005. 'And when I got there, it felt completely natural. Because we were all from the Middle East, different cultures but same temperament, same character.' The only hard part, she says, was playing Wagner, 'the music that was played when Jews were being sent to gas chambers. But I played it, and it was so powerful and beautiful. If it had not been so beautiful, it would not have been so difficult.'
>
> With the Divan, 'we live another reality, a good reality. You make good friends, then you see them next year. You party together—there's no dinner in any restaurant without music and dancing. We play the Beatles, Pearl Jam, Arab and Israeli music, we get our instruments out and play. In Israel, it's impossible for us to hear the other side of the story. I know something about what is happening in Palestine, but it became clearer, more personal. Even more beautiful, though, was when we didn't want to talk about it. When I am playing next to Dana from Syria I don't think, "She's from Syria", I think,"That's my friend Dana." We talked about boys, girls or Mozart. There is a lot of romance.' Between Israelis and Palestinians? 'My friend is with a man from Nazareth, but they had to go and live in Germany. It's very hard to have a relationship between Arabs and Jews, and I don't know of a relationship between an Israeli and someone from Palestine.'[41]

Several research projects in the USA are reported in the USA government document *Champions of Change; the*

Impact of the Arts on Learning.[42] The documents report that among grade 10 students 75% took no part in any kind of music or arts activities, and among grade 12 students, 85% took no part. But the evidence from many thousands of American school students is overwhelming that learning to play an instrument has a significant effect on performance in school subjects generally. Differences in performance in English and mathematics between those in Grade 8 who played instruments and those who did not ranged between 16 and 18% higher in the former. By Grade 12, the difference amounted to 46%. Among comments from school administrators found in the *Champions of Change* document is the following from a middle-school principal:

> You are talking to someone who had very little to do with the arts before I came here. This has changed me enormously. I have an appreciation for the arts that I never had before. I have seen youngsters come through here who perhaps weren't as motivated, and I have seen them take off and fly because we pulled them into an art and opened up new avenues. I couldn't work anymore in a school that wasn't totally immersed in the arts.

Significantly, this report documents the ways in which generalist teachers in primary and middle schools worked collaboratively with specialist music teachers to deliver programs. And since the vast majority of teachers across the English-speaking world are generalists, this use of specialists working with them is a model which should be adopted here in Australia. But first it is necessary for state and territory governments to acknowledge the need for music specialists to be employed in primary schools.

Plato and the mathematical tradition

Musically speaking, the Western art traditions have given the world's music two major and unique capabilities which have fed into our contemporary entertainment world over the last two centuries to become virtually universal, and which distinguish it from the traditional music of other cultures. These are: *the capacity for elements of music, such as melody, harmony, rhythm and instrumentation, to express emotion; and the importance of structure in melody and harmony, based on extrapolations from proportional mathematics which contain powerful aesthetic and cognitive effects*. No other musical culture has evolved in this way, and the potential universality of these attributes is now acknowledged. I do not argue for superiority or for the 'rightness' of Western art music, but rather for its profundity and its ability to deal with human behaviour and our psychology in ways of which no other communication is capable. One of the most important attributes of Western art music is its ability to affect behaviour; and in order to make my case more explicit, I must first outline some origins and intentions of Western art music.

All cultures regard music as possessing special powers capable of changing our emotional state, curing disease, or influencing our behaviour for good or ill. The Western cultural traditions from their very inception are rich in accounts of the power of music. Nearly three thousand years ago, in Book XII of the *Odyssey*, Homer described how Circe, daughter of Helios (the Sun), warns Ulysses about the song of the Sirens.[43] To hear their singing, she warns, is to be drawn to certain death.

> First you will come to the Sirens who enchant all who come near them. If any one unwarily draws in too close and hears the singing of the Sirens, his wife and children will never welcome him home again, for they sit in a green field and warble him to death with the sweetness of their song. There is a great heap of dead men's bones lying all around, with the flesh still rotting off them.

Some four centuries later Plato argued in *The Republic* that since music had such enormous powers, only 'good' music should be used in the education of the young; 'bad' music, which induced immoral, unethical and undesirable behaviour, should be banned.[44]

> Only good melodies and rhythms should be taught to young children, those which contain melodic and rhythmic elements promoting the ideal of the good and noble. . . Good speech, good harmony, good grace, and good rhythm accompany a good disposition, and rhythm and harmony touch the soul directly [. . .] The man who makes the finest mixture of gymnastic with music and brings them to his soul in the most proper measure is the one of whom we would most correctly say that he is the most perfectly musical and well harmonized. (Book II)
>
> Education in music is most sovereign, because more than anything else rhythm and harmony find their way to the inmost soul and take strongest hold upon it. (Book III)

This particular attitude towards music in education, and music in society at large, has permeated the thinking of the West from the early years of

Christianity through to the latter half of the twentieth century.[45]

But how do we bring these wonderful attributes of music to our soul, as Plato wants? We cannot find the answer in Plato's ideal music because he did not identify any melody or rhythm that contained such virtue, wisdom and 'harmony' of body and mind. The answer lies in understanding why and how in the evolution of Western culture these ideals of Plato were made into real music. For Plato the pathway to wisdom was through mathematics, and he referred to the proportional mathematics of the Pythagoreans in his dialogues. He was, in fact, the first to write down the ancient wisdom and knowledge of the Pythagoreans, and it is that source which has inspired successive generations of musicians, poets, philosophers, mathematicians and scientists to discover the secrets to which Plato referred. The story is peppered with illogicalities, untruths, and sometimes nonsense. Nevertheless, from this perhaps unpromising beginning has sprung one of the most powerful semiotic systems of artistic expression seen on the planet.

Modern physics has demonstrated the efficacy of claims made by Plato and Pythagoras about music. The late 18th century mathematician, J.B. Fourier, developed a theorem for calculating the harmonic elements of an ideal vibrating string. This appeared to confirm the beliefs of the Pythagoreans, and Plato's argument, so let me explain briefly how. These elements were whole number multiples of the basic rate of vibration of, say, a violin string, or a column of air in a trumpet. So if, for example, a violin string was vibrating in ideal fashion, which is to say in perfect tune, at 250 times per second (the rate of vibration of middle C) then the harmonics would be 500 (2 X), 750 (3 X), 1000 (4 X), 1250 (5 X), 1500 (6 X), and so on. The point being that these harmonics would be in the ratio of 1:2:3:4 etc., to the basic rate of vibration. Why is this so important to Plato's theory and to the development of Western art music with all the powers I have attributed to it? It was the beginnings of a science of human behaviour explained mathematically. Here was the origin of the idea that certain musical sounds contain specific analogs of human emotion, and that they affect our behaviour, causing empathetic responses when we hear them.

Originally Plato's theory was not really about music, but rather about the nature of the universe and the place of humans within it. He saw the 'harmony' of the heavenly spheres as the desired ideal state of humans: in perfect harmony with themselves and the cosmos.[46] Empirically, the problem was to work out how the planets in the sky did not crash into each other. The answer, said Plato, was this mysterious force he called harmony: a perfect set of relationships described through proportional mathematics which kept them in a close relationship but also apart and spinning in their respective heavenly paths. Music came into it by virtue of the ability to work out ratios between two notes on a single vibrating string, the monochord. By stopping the string in certain places one could produce musical intervals and calculate the mathematical ratios of the two notes. This, said Pythagoras, whom Plato faithfully reported, provided the analogy with the movements of the planets and their relationships to each other.

But Plato also suggested this approach could be used as an empirical justification for identifying through their music the bad or good behaviour of certain tribes around Athens. He gave no specific details of this music, however, and it was left to subsequent scholars and eventually musicians to work out the semiotic system at which Plato hinted. In fact, what was little more than a belief system eventually became a great artistic tradition, linked to all aspects of life. How music became central to human psychology and itself became an art form capable of expressing the whole range of human emotions is a fascinating story.

Pythagorean proportional mathematics was the ancient way to explain what we call gravity.[47] Whole numbers were thought to contain the essence of goodness, especially the series 1:2:3:4. The argument included the following as proof of perfection: 1 plus 2 equals 3; 1 plus 3 equals 4, 1plus 4 equals 2 plus 3, and $1 + 2 + 3 + 4 = 10$, the 'perfect' number, one and zero. The perfect ratios formed by these whole numbers and this movement, as with a vibrating string, must, the argument goes, produce heavenly (or perfect) music: the music of the spheres.

Plato explained how Pythagoras discovered this as he passed a blacksmith's forge and heard the sounds of the hammers which related to each other in these ratios: 2:1, the musical octave, 3:2 the musical 5th, 4:3 the musical 4th. Of course this was nonsense, merely a sort of parable. In any case, it would not be the hammers which produced the sound but the object the hammer struck. Nevertheless, it began one of the great belief systems of the world. By the seventeenth century, European musicians had invented the major and minor key system which is now ubiquitous. The perfect intervals of these scales are the octave (ratio of 2:1), the 4th (4:3) and the 5th (3:2). Other intervals are not perfect because their ratios are outside these perfect four (e.g. the minor 3rd – A to C – had a ratio of 32:27; the major 3rd – C to E – a ratio of 81:64—all outside the efficiency of the 'perfect' intervals.

The following examples illustrate how the use of mathematics to explain and predict both musical expression and human responses to music had become a precise system:

> Small intervals (semitones, minor 3rds) are weak when rising but vigorous when falling;
>
> Large intervals (tone, 4th, 5th, etc.) are vigorous when rising, weak when falling;
>
> The major 3rd is of a lively and happy nature and likes to ascend melodically;
>
> The minor 3rd is feeble and likes to descend.
>
> (Nicholas Valentino, *L'antica Musica ridotto all moderna* Practica (1555))
>
> The 5th ascending is sad, descending is joyous.[48] (Vincenzo Galileo, *Dialogue* (1581)).

René Descartes in *Les passions de l'âme* (1649) argued mathematically for a rational explanation of human responses to various melodic movements, claiming he had found the scientific basis of human emotions. And so began an unquenchable scientific desire to find the answers to the mysteries of musical expression using mathematics and physics which still goes on today in the field of scientific psychology.

That Western culture and the foundations of its art music are based on a belief system posing as science, which in effect constitutes the beginnings of Western scientific thinking, is not, however, the point. The point is that in the West the whole epistemological edifice we call culture seeks to explain, predict, and engulf us in a body of knowledge, which stems from these Mediterranean origins.[49] And only if we can understand our own origins in this way can we stand a chance of understanding those of other cultures.

The purpose of an education is to learn how to access and understand these ancient and long established traditions of enquiry into the human condition. Historically, any culture has evolved such traditions by way of explanation and understanding. The long history of music in the Western traditions is a history of how music sought to fulfil Plato's conditions of expression, the evidence of which lies in the history of opera, symphony, and in fact in all categories of Western art music, particularly from the Renaissance onwards, through to the present and the current uses of music in film, television and all contemporary communications media. We make distinctions between different types of music by virtue of their effects on us. But these effects are a product of hundreds of years of intellectual and musical development, not something which occurs by chance or suddenly. An education implies an understanding of such traditions.

The development of education in the West continued to use Plato and the educative effects of music from its medieval origins until the mid-twentieth century.[50] At this point, dramatically, a significant change occurred: the arrival of manufactured music.

6

African-American music and the arrival of pop

Technological innovation introduced to Western society the music known as jazz, quickly labelled the music of the devil by religious and political leaders, because of its overt and perceived sexuality and its 'primitive' African-American origins. Plato was cited as the moral and musical justification for banning such music.

An African-American form of Blues music, rock 'n roll, burst from its relative obscurity in the Southern states of the USA to capture the hearts and minds of young people across the globe. To some this occurrence was a shock; to others it signalled more evidence of the immense power of music to attract people—this time, some argued, with more seductive and dangerous consequences. The Western expressive traditions in art music became the model for criticism.

Like a tidal wave, the commercial entertainment media proclaimed, the sounds of the 19-year-old Elvis Presley, a white boy from Memphis, singing the black music he grew up with, and gyrating his hips on television and in the movies, swept across the Western world. In the USA during the 1950s a number of State legislatures banned Elvis from even setting foot in their territory, while in Europe, the UK in particular, and in Australia, church and political leaders railed against this 'blasphemous' form of popular music and dance, warning that the end of civilization was at hand and calling for control. The old Platonic beliefs about good and evil music were shaken to their core. How could such music gain such popularity among the young so quickly? And what was the source of its power, its hold over people? There are recordings of television shows in the USA filmed during the late 1950s and early 1960s showing Elvis performing to family audiences of mums, dads and children much to their delight, but by this time he was no longer an icon for disenchanted youth.

Often forgotten in light of the cult of youth which evolved at this time, is the fact that during the use of the popular music recording industry between the 1940s and the 1960s there were music and film stars far more popular than Elvis ever was, and many performed music which had more affinity with art music than with the new style of rock/pop. And this refers to popular music across society and age groups.

Mario Lanza, often referred to as the American Caruso, became internationally famous through movies like *The Great Caruso* in the early 1950s. His operatic singing on film was sensational. His appeal affected all ages and all continents. Popular singing film stars Doris Day and Frank Sinatra had enduring global followers. The crooner Bing Crosby had a lifetime career of movie hits and his film *White Christmas* and the song of the same name held top spots throughout the world at Christmas time right through until the late 1970s and beyond.

Later in the 1950s the succession of Broadway musicals on stage and on film captured many millions of fans: *Showboat*, *South Pacific* and *Carousel* were all more popular than any movie Elvis made. Their music filled the radio waves the world over. And the 1965 movie, *The Sound of Music*, was easily the most popular film of the whole period; over the years its music has sold more recordings than Elvis, the Beatles, or any other pop/rock group since. The rise to prominence of pop/rock stars needs to be seen in the context of a wider definition of popular music. But also, more pragmatically, as argued by Cambridge social historian David Fowler, most pop stars were merely entrepreneurs out to make as much money as possible from very young mesmerized fans, mostly girls aged 10–14. [51]

In rock 'n roll meaning appears more in the gesture of the singer/dancer than in the music. There was, and indeed is now, no taxonomy of expressive meanings in rock/pop such as there is in classical music, yet so powerful has been the intrusion of the Western art music traditions into pop/rock, that most fans believe this music can also express feelings, emotions, and psychological states as powerfully as any operatic aria. The origins of rock in the African-American traditions do not lie in this type of expressiveness, however. African-American music is essentially movement and dance music, and its expressiveness lies in its communal significance, not in the expression of an individual emotional drama. In the pop/rock traditions where assimilation of Western expressiveness has occurred, the singer can make any musical element mean what s/he wants it to mean but only through visual and aural gesture. This is not the case with Western art music where meaning lies in the sounds themselves and how effectively the performer expresses them.

It is true that historically this meaning was exclusive to the aristocratic and politically powerful. It was the music of the élite, for sure, but the twentieth century and all the developments in communications media, especially the cinema, have made such music accessible to all.

Which creates a dilemma for the musically literate. Audiences need no preparation time to enjoy popular music; and the mass production of music has led to us treating art music in a similarly cavalier way. But classical music takes time to fully appreciate, is difficult to understand, and requires technical competence and cognitive ability acquired through education and experience. The rewards are those of greater understanding of, and empathy with, the human predicament. This is an important issue for education. Pop/rock is designed for immediate appeal and this diminishes as the fans look for new sensations.

The *National Review of School Music Education* is now four years old and so far, despite all the evidence, no action has been taken on its recommendations. This is not an issue simply of musical literacy but of our shameful failure to take advantage of an essential tool in the teaching of those recognized 'core learning areas': mathematics, literacy and languages. Never mind the education of a civilised society.

7

Conclusion

The *National Review* drew the following conclusions:

- In general terms there is a lack of consistent quality in music education and a lack of consistency in the provision of music education.
- For some students, no formal music education is provided; for others, music education is fragmentary, delivered non-continuously and lacking the sequential development that is so critical for a solid grounding in music.
- Music is sometimes taught by teachers who are ill prepared to do so.
- In general, school systems and sectors give low priority and status to music in schools.
- This, in turn, demonstrates a need for leadership and action in response to what some have described as 'a crisis' for Australian school music education. (p. 106)

Responses from submissions to the *Review* and surveys undertaken by the *Review* suggest that opportunities for young people to engage and participate in music in schools have declined over the past two decades. There appear to be a number of contributing factors to this apparent decline.

- The first is the crowded curriculum and the increasing demands on schools to meet an ever widening array of topics. In this context, music is sometimes given lower priority or even lost from the curriculum. In particular, the sustained continuity that is essential to support sequential, developmental learning in music (as necessary in music as in other subjects) has been severely affected.
- A second and related factor is the impact of the ongoing succession of reforms in curriculum. While recognition of the Arts Learning Area was welcomed in general, the trend to general 'arts' outcomes—and, in some States, cross-curricular outcomes—is contributing to a drift away from music education.
- A third factor is revealed in a number of submissions and other reports, where many K–10 generalist classroom teachers cite their lack of training in music teaching as contributing factors to their inability to implement and maintain effective music programs. Furthermore, there has been an erosion of system support. (p. 106)

The *Review*'s findings indicate that, in most states and territories, curriculum support such as advisory teachers and, in particular, on-going professional development have been withdrawn, re-directed or depleted. In addition, in some states syllabus and support documents are out of date or written in ways that no longer provide direct guidance to teachers, particularly inexperienced teachers. This further compounds the reported lack of competence and confidence on the part of many generalist teachers about teaching music. Difficulties in staffing music in schools and associated problems with teacher education combine to limit the effectiveness of music education in schools. A further factor is that of funding. (pp. 106-7)

The *Review* urges the Australian Government and State and Territory governments to:

- assert the value of music education for all Australian students
- place immediate priority on improving and sustaining the quality and status of music education
- provide sufficient funding to support effective, quality music education that is accessible to all Australian children and addresses the specific areas detailed in this *Review*. (p. 107)

In order to achieve these priorities the *Review* proposes fifteen courses of action:

1. enhance the status of school music education (p. 109)
2. ensure every Australian child has opportunities to participate and engage in continuous sequential, developmental music education programmes (p. 111)
3. improve the standard of pre-service music

education for all generalist classroom teachers (p. 113)

4. improve the quality, and expand the provision, of pre-service music education courses for specialist classroom teachers (p. 117)
5. ensure that Australian primary and K–10 generalist classroom teachers can support music education; and, primary and secondary specialist music teachers can develop and maintain their knowledge, understanding, skills and values about teaching music (p. 119)
6. support a cohesive inclusive curriculum approach to music education that meets student needs and interests (p. 123)
7. ensure that every Australian student participates and engages in initial instrumental music programmes; and students with identified interest and talent in instrumental music are provided with sustained instrumental music programmes (p. 127)
8. ensure that every Australian student participates and engages in initial vocal music programmes; and students with identified interest and talent in vocal music are provide with sustained vocal music programmes (p. 128)
9. ensure that music technology is actively included in the curriculum (p. 129)
10. ensure provision of the facilities and equipment necessary for every Australian student to participate and engage in continuous, sequential, developmental music education programmes (p. 130)

11. ensure that music in schools is supported and enhanced by partnerships with key music and arts funding organisations (p. 131)
12. recognise the crucial role of school leadership in successful music education in schools (p. 133)
13. ensure all primary school students have access to music specialist teachers (p. 136)
14. ensure sufficient time for continuous developmental music programmes for all students K–10 (p. 138)
15. demonstrate quality music programmes through appropriate accountability measures (p. 140).

There is no doubt that if all the above recommendations are acted upon by all levels of government, music in Australian schools will be immeasurably improved. However, there remains one omission. *Nowhere in the Review is any composition recommended for study, performance or appreciation.* In the light of the research evidence presented, I would add a sixteenth imperative: *that all Australian students learn some major works of the Western classical art traditions.* To leave out the actual content of music education, as the *Review* does, is an abrogation, and reflects a mindset fearful of stating where our values lie. Other countries are not so fearful and list those pieces of Western art music they believe to be essential to an education. It would be tragic if all the *Review*'s recommendations were followed, and all the resources provided, and yet Australian music education was still confined, by teacher discretion, to performing and listening to pop music.

Endnotes

1. *National Review of School Music Education* (DEST, 2005), hereafter referred to simply as the *Review*. The report, authored by a team led by Robin Pascoe, can be found at http://www.dest.gov.au/sectors/school_education/policy_initiatives_reviews/reviews/school_music_education/
2. See Gary MacPherson, 'Crisis: the Serious State of Music Education in Australian Schools', *Music Forum*, 1 (1995), p. 45.
3. See *Critical Links: Learning in the Arts and Student Social and Academic Development*, available from the Arts Education Partnership website at http://aep-arts.org/cllinkspage.htm (accessed 13 January 2009). The project was sponsored by the National Endowment for the Arts and the US Department of Education. The contributing researchers were Karen Bradley (dance), James Catterall (drama & transfer of learning), Larry Scripp (music), Terry Baker (visual arts), and Rob Horowitz (multi-arts).
4. *Arts Education Partnership of Washington DC* website: http://aep-arts.org/cllinkspage.htm (accessed 25 September 2005).
5. *Ibid*.
6. Reported in the *Guardian*, UK, at http://www.guardian.co.uk/education/2006/sep/20/schools/uk (accessed 19 November 2008).
7. *Ibid*.

8 See http://mca.org.au/index.php?id=202

9 http://www.medicalnewstoday.com/articles/65148.php

10 Olive Wetter, Frantz Koerner & Adrian Schwaninger, 'Does musical training improve school performance?', *Instructional Science* (in press: 2009), see http://sprinterlink.com/content/e77p01286573155/ (accessed 10 February 2009).

11 QCA website: http://www.qca.org.uk/artsalive/why_invest (accessed 21 September 2005).

12 *Ibid.*

13 BBC News announcement: http://newsvote.bbc.co.uk_news/educ (accessed 25 January 2009).

14 BBC News item: 'Music vital to school standards', 25 January 2009, at BBC website: http://newsvote.bbc.co.uk/mpapps/pagetools/print/news.bbc.co.uk/2/hi/uk_news/educ (accessed 30 January 2009).

15 See Music Manifesto website at http://www.musicmanifesto.co.uk/news/details/Music-partnerships-projects-news-bids

16 Statistics in this and the following paragraph are taken from the Independent Schools Council of Australia website: http://isce.edu.au/html/stats/school (accessed 16 January 2009).

17 See the NSW Department of Education and Training website at: http://www.det.nsw.edu.au/media/downloads/reports_stats/statsbulletin/stat2007.pdf (accessed 16 January 2009).

18 These would include the following, to name only a few: Abottsleigh, St Andrews Cathedral School, Barker College, Kings School, Knox Grammar, MLC Burwood, SCEGS Darlinghurst, SCEGS Redlands, Shore School, Sydney Grammar School, Tara School, Trinity Grammar School and Wenona School.

19 'Music instruction in pre-service training of classroom teachers', *Music Forum*, 13 (2007), p. 26.

20 See http://www.boardofstudies.nsw.edu.au (accessed 17 January 2009).

21 Available at http:/www.det.wa.edu.au/content/syllabus (accessed 18 January 2009).

22 *Ibid*.

23 See Queensland Education website, at http://www.qsa.qld.edu.au/download/syllabus/music_04_guide.pdf (accessed 18 January 2009).

24 *Ibid*.

25 Prominent among the publications which focused on how people use music in their daily lives are Simon Frith, *Performing Rites: On the Value of Popular Music* (Cambridge, MA: Harvard University Press, 1996); Tia DeNora, *Music in Everyday Life* (Cambridge: CUP, 2000); John Connell & Chris Gibson, *sound tracks: popular music, identity and place* (London: Routledge, 2003); Raymond MacDonald, David Hargreaves & Dorothy Miell (eds), *Musical Identities* (Oxford: OUP, 2002) and Christopher Small, *Musicking: The Meanings of Performing and Listening* (Hanover, NH & London: University Press of New England, 1998).

26 See, in particular, Pierre Bourdieu, 'The school as a conservative force: scholastic and cultural inequalities', in *Contemporary Research in the Sociology of Education*, ed. by John Eggleston (London: Methuen, 1974) and 'Cultural reproduction and social reproduction', in *Power and Ideology in Education*, ed. by Jerome Karabel & A.H. Halsey (London: Methuen, 1977).

27 The Birmingham Group of sociologists and cultural theorists produced a number of seminal texts including Paul Willis, *Profane Culture* (London: Routledge, 1978) and Stuart Hall, 'Deviance, politics and the media',

in Paul Rock & Mary Macintosh (eds), *Deviance and Social Control* (London: Tavistock Publications, 1997), pp. 261–305.

28 See, in particular, Freire's widely-influential *Pedagogy of the Oppressed* (New York: Herder & Herder, 1970).

29 See, for example, Ivan Illich, *Deschooling Society* (New York: Harper & Row, 1971).

30 The 1966 Education Act was intended to abolish selection for secondary education in the UK.

31 Because I had been Director of Music in a Queen Elizabeth Grammar School, a King Edward VIth Grammar School and King's School, the newly-appointed head of this school, a very young man, sarcastically asked if I only taught in schools with royal names. He had no interest at all in the music I had got children to perform (or which had attracted the children to the school) only my views on sociological issues in education. To him music did not matter.

32 During my time as Chief Examiner for Music for the International Baccalaureate Organisation, I saw the success of transforming one USA High School in Chicago, Lincoln Park High. The move by parents, teachers, business and others to transform the school into a zero-tolerance IBO school worked well. Students had no choice but to work hard, conform and contribute—or leave. Within a few years many Ivy League universities were offering scholarships to Lincoln Park students at grade 12. This was a fine example of integrating poor African-American students into the mainstream,

33 Courtney Cazden and others, 'A pedagogy of multiliteracies: designing social futures', *Harvard Educational Review*, 66 (1996), pp. 60–93.

34 See Allan Luke, 'Critical literacy in Australia', *Journal of Adolescent and Adult Literacy*, 43 (2000), pp. 448–61.

35 For example, an ARC-funded project by academics from the Universities of Queensland and Newcastle in 2000, led by Allan Luke, had important effects in both Queensland and New South Wales schools and on educational thinking.

36 Douwe Draaisma, *Metaphors of Memory: A History of Ideas About the Mind* (Cambridge: CUP, 2000) and *Why Life Speeds Up As You Get Older: How Memory Shapes our Past* (Cambridge: CUP, 2004).

37 For example, the 2003 winner, Guy Sebastian, had studied music for many years prior to entering *Idol*. Casey Donovan, winner in 2004, was a student at the Australian Institute of Music in Sydney. The runner-up that year was Anthony Callea, a long-time music student, who began training as a classical musician.

38 Countries like South Korea, Japan, and China have centralised national curricula which all schools are obliged to follow. These contain considerable details of content, including specific pieces of Western art music which all children, at specified stages of their development, are expected to learn, listen to and know about.

39 Sheila Melvin & Jingdon Cai, *Rhapsody in Red: How Western Classical Music Became Chinese* (New York: Algora, 2004).

40 See http://makeartlikeyoucare.blogspot.com/2008/04/el-systema-changing-world-through-music.html (accessed 30 January 2009).

41 Ed Vuillamy, 'Bridging the gap', *Observer*, 13 July 2008, available at http://www.guardian.co.uk/music/2008/jul/13/classicalmusicandopera.israelandthepalestinians (accessed 6 February 2009).

42 *Champions of Change: The Impact of the Arts on Learning*, ed. by Edward B. Fiske (The GE Fund & the John D. & Catherine T. MacArthur Foundation, 2000).

43 Homer's epic poems, the *Iliad* and the *Odyssey,* became important ethical, moral and psychological foundations for Western civilisation. Circe gives her gruesome warning in Book XII of the *Odyssey*, explaining that the Sirens sit in a green field and warble the unwary to death with the sweetness of their song.

44 Plato's argument in *The Republic* linked certain music to particular tribes, arguing that those tribes which were known for their illiberal and immoral habits had developed music which contained the essence of these undesirable behaviours. On the other hand, tribes with more desirable behaviours had developed more morally and ethically desirable music. The mere act of performing either type of music would induce the associated behaviour.

45 Vittorino da Feltre (1378-1446) introduced listening to good music at mealtimes for his students in Mantua. But see William Harrison Woodward, *Studies in Education during the Age of the Renaissance, 1400-1600* (Cambridge: CUP, 1906), and John Adamson, *A Short History of Education* (Cambridge: CUP, 1919) and Robert Walker, *Music Education: Cultural Values, Social Change and Innovation* (Springfield, ILL: Charles C. Thomas, 2007) for a fuller coverage of music in education through the ages.

46 It is interesting to note here how Platonism had a major impact on the early development of Christianity, but this it is outside the scope of this paper.

47 See Walker, *Music Education*.

48 For a fuller discussion of Plato's claims about music and how they live on today, see Walker, *Music Education*.

49 In fact, the use of proportional mathematics to tune musical intervals dates back to China several hundred years before Pythagoras lived. It is well established that Pythagoras derived his mystical beliefs about numbers

in large measure from the ancient Chinese. On this see Robert Walker, *Musical Beliefs: Psycho-acoustic, Mythic and Educational* (NY: Columbia University Teachers College Press, 1990).

50 See Walker, *Music Education*, for a summary of the role of music in education over the last thousand years. Music was used in this period throughout Europe to civilise, to engender good behaviour and to induce good attitudes to education.

51 David Fowler, *Youth Culture in Modern Britain, c.1920-c.1970* (London: Palgrave MacMillan, 2008).

Readers' Forum

Responses to Peter Rechniewski's *On the Permanent Underground: Australian Contemporary Jazz in the New Millenium*, (Platform Papers 16)

Louise Denson is Head of Jazz Studies at the Queensland Conservatorium. A pianist and composer/arranger, she has performed extensively with various jazz and latin ensembles..

Here it comes, the dreaded Jazz Area Open Day question: 'What kind of a job will Johnny/Janey be able to get if s/he gets a degree in jazz?'

And the never-voiced reply: 'Accountancy and plumbing are professions which attract six-figure incomes, and after only a few years of post-jazz-degree training, Johnny/Janey can be gainfully employed, playing jazz on the weekends for fun.'

Peter Rechniewski's examination (PP16) of low levels of public funding and lamentable media coverage goes a long way towards explaining why 'improvising musician' is not currently a viable career choice in Australia. Of more immediate concern than career advancement for the gigging musician, however, is how little they are going to be paid this very weekend at the local watering hole for their professional services.

Several factors conspire to keep musicians' wages low in the commercial market: for example, music is often an add-on after every other expense has been budgeted for and therefore needs to be low cost. Then there's the notion that musicians love what they do so much they don't need to be paid. But how do the musicians themselves contribute to this situation? The fact is that they agree to play for substandard wages, in unacceptable conditions. Why do they do it? Can they do anything on their own behalf to improve their lot?

One key factor is that jazz musicians do not have a professional association, a union or a guild which adequately represents their interests. Musicians' unions tend to concentrate their efforts on musicians who have full-time positions with large organisations. Orchestral musicians, for example, have wages and conditions of work determined by the Symphony Orchestra Musicians' Agreement (SOMA), administered by the Media Entertainment Arts Alliance (MEAA).

Most jazz musicians, on the other hand, would not be able to say what conditions govern their employment, nor what their minimum wage should be, nor even what state award might apply to them. Probably few of them have ever looked into membership in a union or professional association which would set higher minimums for their labour.

But supposing that all jazz musicians joined such an organisation? How would it help them when negotiating a gig at the local pub? Said organisation would need a mechanism for enforcing minimum wages and conditions for its members, or else the musicians would soon feel they were paying their dues for nothing. This was certainly the case when I lived in Montreal, where a strong American Federation of Musicians' branch was largely ignored by jazz musicians. The casual gigging scene was deemed too hard to regulate, so free-lancers were left to their own devices, working for whatever wages a venue would pay.

And that, of course, is part of the problem: jazz musicians tend to play for whatever wages a venue will pay, because they want to play and there just aren't that many opportunities. So even if they had an organisation representing their interests, chances are they themselves would ignore the agreed-upon minimums and play anyway.

The image of the jazz musician in popular culture is that of the misunderstood genius, the outsider to the music establishment, the heroic loner who spends thousands of hours developing a personal voice and pursuing a musical and spiritual ideal ... These things may all be true—indeed, they often are true—but the emphasis on the individual most certainly serves to undermine any notions of collective action toward better employment conditions in the sector.

So what can we do, as gigging musicians, about this state of affairs?

We can inform ourselves about laws, statutes and awards which govern our sector.

We can investigate associations and organisations which claim to represent our interests as gigging musicians. We can join the ones that actually do, and ask the ones that don't what the incentive might be to join if we don't see ourselves in their literature. We can also join advocacy groups such as, here in Brisbane, Jazz Queensland and Q Music, and become part of the public debate.

We can discuss what is going on in our local scenes, including rates of pay and conditions. This could prevent the inadvertent undercutting of wages which occurs when a new band on the scene doesn't know what the going rates are at a certain venue. Similarly, we should tell musicians who are deliberately undercutting other bands just to get the gig, how destructive that behaviour is for everyone on the scene. Given that many entertainment managers can't distinguish a musical silk purse from a sow's ear, they will always go for the cheaper option and then it's very difficult to recover lost ground.

Any of us who are also active in the organisation of festivals and events can ask for higher wages per musician in grant applications. We may not get it: but we need to start asking, and keep asking over and over again.

Any of us who are teaching—and most of us are!—can talk to our students about the scene and emphasize that even though they are students, if they are supplying a professional service they should be paid a professional wage. Again, potential employers will go for the cheaper option if they can, and the whole scene suffers for it.

And lastly, we can support one another when someone is brave enough to make a stand against a venue offering unacceptable wages or conditions. Recently a Brisbane club with a long-running low-paid gig tried to lower musicians' wages by no longer supplying a sound technician: they proposed that the musicians should hire one out of their wages if they needed this service. Word travelled round the community overnight, and several bands told the venue they would no longer be available to play under those conditions. Within a few days the venue had decided that they could afford the sound technician after all and conditions were back to normal.

I look forward to the day that I can assure a worried parent at Jazz Area Open Day that Johnny or Janey will enjoy a rewarding career and live a comfortable and decent life as an improvising musician in Australia. That day may be a long way off, but we in the jazz community can ensure it arrives sooner rather than later if we take responsibility individually and collectively for our own well-being.

Fax this form to Currency House Inc. at: 02 9319 3649

Or post to: Currency House Inc., PO Box 2270, Strawberry Hills NSW 2012 Australia